T0208398

A
Poetic Compilation
Of
Life's Realities

A
POETIC COMPILATION
OF
LIFE'S REALITIES

UNCERTAINTIES OF LIFE
VOLUME 1

ROLLIN G. MERCURIUS

Library of Congress Control Number:		2021905314
ISBN:	Hardcover	978-1-6641-6326-3
	Softcover	978-1-6641-6325-6
	eBook	978-1-6641-6324-9

Print information available on the last page.

Rev. date: 03/11/2021

To order additional copies of this book, contact:
Xlibris
844-714-8691
www.Xlibris.com
Orders@Xlibris.com
826699

CONTENTS

To my mom, Annie Mae Dyer (October 14, 1912–February 25, 2007)

She was my first teacher, whose uncanny wisdom, vision, and knowledge has helped to sustain lives in our family, extended family, and acquaintances. Many individuals have traveled thousands of miles to seek her advice and counseling, never leaving disappointed, expressing profound appreciation and gratitude.

EXPECT ANYTHING FROM ANYONE AT ANYTIME,
AS YOU NEVER KNOW WHAT A PERSON MAY
SAY OR DO WHEN IT'S CONVENIENT.

ACKNOWLEDGMENTS

I first give thanks to the Almighty Father for his grace, loving-kindness, and for his guidance and protection in all aspects of my life, without which this project would be impossible.

These works would not have been completed without the effort and understanding of gifted people, whose thoughts and perspective played an integral role in bringing it to fruition.

I wish to thank my beautiful wife, Marjorie; children, Sheronette, Vivette, Karlene (Cess) Tremayne, Tanika, Trevena, Xavier, Kristoff, and Raheim; grandchildren, Quewana Blake, Jovani White, Nya Griffiths, Nalani Griffiths, and Nehemiah Griffiths; and great-grandchild Rylee Thomas.

To Ambrozene "Cherry" Epo, my sister, who has been an immeasurable source of continued inspiration, and to Dr. Conrad Dyer, I convey appreciation for constantly encouraging me to document my thoughts and experiences over the years.

You all have been my inspiration, and I thank you.

To the Allman Town community in Kingston, Jamaica, where I grew up, guided by the teachings of stalwarts Jeremiah "Miah" Carr, the first Rastafarian with whom I interacted, and Winston "Dada" Allen, my mentor. Pastor of Saint Matthews Church, the Reverend Weeville Gordon, whose spiritual guidance sustained the community. Also of critical importance was Vincent "Buckles" Henry of Rosemary Lane "Southside" Kingston, all from whom I learned different aspects of the "streets" where the molding of my existence was formulated.

I am forever grateful.

UNAPOLOGETIC

This is who I am created by the Father
Molded by man, enlightened by elders
A prime example debunking the myth
The company you keep determines your societal fit
Values adopted, taught by streetwise mercenaries
Reminiscent of Christ on choosing his disciples
Who sought his flock from those deemed undesirable

Having taken a stand against being divided and ruled
Sought instead to be uplifted and schooled
Having taken a stand against tyranny and mayhem
Rejected hypocrisy manifested by the heathen
Having taken a stand against all deceptive practices
Sought to be truthful and honest in all instances

Seen as a youth with good ethical traits
Expectations of being able to suppress and hold down
Negative thoughts and actions reared on the stomping ground
By quick-tempered, ignorant, and violent brothers
Whose ultimate aim was to eliminate others
A means projecting their dark misguided prowess
Leaving families and loved ones consumed with distress
Having no compassion for who got hurt in the process

Embracing the philosophy of rejecting crime
Expecting anything from anyone at any given time
As you never know what a person will say or do
When it's convenient to do so, which rings true
With backs pushed up against the wall
Man will spill his guts so as not to take the fall
Throwing even his own brother under the bus
As a matter of survival when confronted with duress

Exhibiting the ability to elevate the youth
Who displayed potential in sports and educational growth
Willing to sacrifice while pushing for opportunities
In otherwise inaccessible private and government entities
Through the goodwill and generosity of valued acquaintances
Whose input was most times truly invaluable
Formalizing the groundwork, making it attainable
For at-risk youth to become upstanding citizens

Ostracized for noninvolvement with a political side
Which would have led to unwarranted social divide
Among childhood friends who only sought to thrive
By any means necessary, having the will to survive
Mitigated decisions that could have had deadly consequences
Sought instead to have peaceful inferences
Facilitated by the wisdom of learned knowledgeable elders
Guided through dangerous tracks by genuine well-wishers

LIFE IS JUST A MOMENT
love your life
life
LIVE IT · LOVE IT · ENJOY IT

Uncertainties of Life

Uncertainties of life may not easily be measured
These may lead to situations that are indeed tethered
Unable to quantify the possibilities that exist
Leads to the notion of not being able to predict
That which there was no need to contend with
Requiring a detailed proactive thought process
Engaging the mind with an assortment of what-ifs

Uncertainties of life everyone will face
Can only be overcome by the Father's grace
Uncertainties of life have different effects
From person to person whose life it affects
Uncertainties of life are devastating to some
While others are blessed with a positive outcome

Having been taught to nurture your own
Maintaining your focus determines how you've grown
Still falling short of the goals you had set
Uncertainties of life spurning hurtful regret
Creating self-doubt of your true potential
Requiring an assessment of your adapted proverbial
Determining the semblance to successful counterparts
Revising your ideas, initiating a new start

Plan as you may with the best of intention
Unforeseen events require changes and modification
There is no guarantee of securing the outcome
Of achieving that which was originally envisioned
It is noteworthy implementing a change of course
Does not guarantee attention from the source
Be that as it may, success will come in due course

The knowledge gained from daily living
At times generates real doubts and creates misgivings
Here today and gone tomorrow
Gives rise to thoughts of life as being borrowed
With no awareness of what sustains each other
Bewildered by the demise of your beloved brother
Each life is determined by the person who lives it
The facts only known if they decide to share it

THE SYSTEM

There are without doubt sinister plans for the youths
Becoming ensnared in the corrupt corrections system
With private prisons established as a major investment
Requiring a commitment from states and government
To ensure beds provided are constantly occupied
By any means necessary, which can be verified
They benefit and are rewarded through infinite greed
By the pain and suffering of vulnerable kids in need

The current system of youth incarnation
Continues daily with scant recognition
Countless lives are callously destroyed
And may never in a lifetime ever be restored
Always remember the youth of today
Will eventually be world leaders of tomorrow

Steps have been taken at the elementary level
Should parents decide to administer the paddle
Kids are encouraged to call the authorities
And have them arrested and promptly incarcerated
Parents have become intimidated and scared
Opting to overlook their destructive behavior
Praying instead for intervention from the Savior

Many kids now knowing their parents' mindset
Have become emboldened, behaving without regret
Operating with impunity, not caring of the consequences
Through actions restricting positive growth in all instances
Knowing underdeveloped minds are at that stage
Being no fault of their own due to tender age
The downward spiral to certain incarceration
Manifests itself with little or no distinction

The trend of misdeeds, disrespect, and intolerance
Displayed by these kids with disdain and arrogance
Curtails the learning process through abject ignorance
Now a prime candidate for introduction to the system
Bouncing around institutions in the interim
Eventually assigned with lengthy incarceration
Fulfilling the conceived plans, expectations, and aspirations
Of people in high places of power and position

The cycle continues through many generations
Where families are targeted with the selection of one
Working-class or poor, the system does not care
Most rich families however can avoid being ensnared
As this corrupt system is strategically designed
With poor families and the least fortunate in mind
Just be aware your skin color does not matter
Educate your children about the realities of the latter

BLESSINGS

Blessings, bestowed by the Father on all humanity
Are not earned by deeds or pretense of humility
Given freely to every person in spite of their wickedness
Through his forever grace and loving-kindness
Most times taken for granted on the pretext of not knowing
Evidenced daily in the process of growing
Conveniently ignored most times deliberately
Expression of innocence voiced loud and aggressively

Convey blessings when greeting one another
Elevating the spirit of your sisters and brothers
Convey blessings in reaching out to those who malign you
Always remember they are in need of blessing too
Convey blessings to those who serve ensuring our safety
Remember the sacrifice being made by their family

Blessings, if measured, are seemingly uneven
From person to person, distributed for a reason
With no set time frame or designated season
Some persons appear to be more blessed than others
In the eyes of the beholder, not necessarily your brother
There are those whose blessings are obvious to behold
While others enjoy hidden blessings limitless and untold
The fortunes of the latter are better than pure gold

The blessing of good health is not guaranteed to all
Genetics being the main factor, determining who falls
The choice of lifestyle also plays a significant role
As communicable diseases are spread, taking a toll
Ravaging humanity, ending countless lives
Curtailing the blessing and associated good vibes
Good health should not be taken for granted
For what it's worth, work to have this blessing consecrated

Blessings used to elevate the Father's agenda
Speak volumes in reversing the action of the diaspora
Assisting his people to be repatriated at long last
To the Motherland Africa correcting atrocities of the past
Where wise men and women of yesteryear
Had sacrificed their lives many without fear
By the teachings and examples that caused their demise
Enlightening the masses who choose to reside

The blessing of children is the greatest of all
Those not afforded that privilege are not exempt at all
The option of parenting those not biologically theirs
Through the adoption process utilized by peers
That blessing may be had, by the love and caring shown
Nurturing these children, providing a loving, structured home

MISDIRECTION

Successful living is determined by a choice of direction
Misdirection being the act of providing false information
With resulting paths taken leading to oblivion
This speaks to life in general or segments of it
Prompting a person on recognition of the error to quit
Caught in time may eventually be corrected
Changing courses of action as was formerly projected
Enacting corrective measures, desired results determined

Misdirection is a scourge, most times a deliberate ploy
Eyes wide open, it is designed to destroy
Misdirection can control and determine life's achievement
Sometimes it requires surrendering to appeasement
Misdirection is life's greatest stumbling block
With devastating precision, trying to turn back the clock
Misdirection must be recognized, neutralizing its effect
To avoid living a life consumed by regret

The choice of faith may be initiated by misdirection
Having been influenced by false and persistent indoctrination
Encouraged by someone or a practicing organization
Driven by a self-serving financially motivated agenda
The maximizing of numbers being their collective idea
Ensuring a robust tithing congregation at all times
Oblivious of the fact families are existing on dimes

The act of loving unfortunately suffers the most
Used as a means to achieve an end from coast to coast
With expressions of love being false in nature
Breaking hearts, destroying lives and, by extension, the future
Of countless poor souls who by trusting became ensnared
Sometimes by being gullible, believing everything they heard
Not to be blamed however for being trusting and vulnerable
Misdirection and deception making life unbearable

Careers are not exempt from being touched by misdirection
When promises made do not come to fruition
Where upward trajectory seems not to be forthcoming
Under the guise of your not being in good standing
Even though all rules and standards are constantly met
Leaving no option but to express profound regret
Of placing confidence where there should have been none
The proof found in the pudding when all is said and done

The choice of sexuality may be a result of misdirection
When young impressionable minds are influenced by association
Sometimes with a person not having the deliberate intention
But whose lifestyle was observed as endearing and attractive
Unaware of the scrutiny, attention, and objective
Of the person whose admiration has now become addictive
Through no fault of theirs, however, advances must be rejected
As the affection being shown was completely unwarranted

FAMILY

Family, decreed by the Father, confirmed by birth
Relations remain the same all over this earth
Most times blessed with awesome family members
Always lending support to chosen endeavors
Sometimes operating under challenging circumstances
Requiring thoughtful consideration, depending on the instance
The resulting decision invariably positive
Cementing the family's overall objective

Family is essential, the backbone of society
Supersedes everything in all of humanity
Family dictates the acquiring of true values
The cornerstone of character is paying your dues
Family nurtures and guarantees proper upbringing
From birth and throughout the process of living

Family sticks together, through good times and bad
Irrespective of differences they previously had
Knowing intimate details concerning recent developments
Letting good sense prevail, alleviating the predicament
In life there always will come that time
When the need is greatest for that additional dime
Friends and acquaintances may show some concern
Family will ensure, you're not being burned

FAMILY CONT'D

In life, however, there is the reality
When convenience dictates the actions of family
Having a need, making use of an opportunity
Initiating deceptive practices to acquire what they need
Sometimes out of desperation, not necessarily of greed
Being up-front and honest would have been best
Cards on the table justifying a request
Of needed assistance with a genuine behest

Family, where life begins and love never ends
Enhancing quality of life, circumventing popular trends
With lives on the line that is no joke
Defending family values, going all for broke
Be it close family or distant relative
The same rings true, the response is decisive
The well-being of family members is seen as priority
Ensuring strong family units within the community

CHARACTER

Character, the determining factor confirming one's standing
in life
Denotes upstanding stature, which is devoid of rife
Projecting honesty and integrity in abundance
Your word being your bond in every instance
Exhibiting copious intelligence, thoughtful and informative
Always seeking positive advancement, which is indicative
Of a proactive mindset with ideas that are productive
With intent and actions never ever subjective

Character is life's main determining factor
Which makes your existence really matter
Character takes precedence over popularity
There is no question of this being the reality
Character is the trait that guarantees progress
Exercised at all times fosters continued success

Character must always be foremost in mind
Reputation serves only to get you in a bind
Your character is who you really are
Reputation is what others think you are
People reveal only what they want you to see
Carefully concealing traits of who they may really be
Character is the vehicle that guarantees your success
Reputation and popularity only serve to impress

CHARACTER Cont'd

Never undermine your character for material gain
A shattered mirror can never be made whole again
Strength of character prevents moments of weakness
Where temptation seeks a foothold, to elevate loneliness
Fostering unwanted discord in relationships
With mutually damaging and degrading conflicts
From which couples never seem able to recover
Bemoaning the probability of being apart forever

Character assassination rears its ugly head
When jealousy and bad mind take precedence instead
Designed to inflict as much damage as possible
With corrosive statements, which were considered unthinkable
The intention being destroying your good character
Retarding your progress as the determining factor
Try as they may by exercising strength of will
This too shall pass, overcoming their efforts still

WISDOM

A favorite phrase of all generations
Experience teaches wisdom, there is no distinction
Wise men seek knowledge and understanding
Foolish men crave material things, having no bearing
On the Father's plan of eternal living
Wisdom is the key that sets us apart
Applied with compassion, avoids fellow man's wrath
Be that it may determine the future
Of mankind's existence in this dispensation

Got to seek God first, then wisdom after
It's the only sure way to avoid disaster
Got to seek wisdom, next make it a priority
Securing the future of your entire family
Wisdom is life, got to make it a surety
The only sure way to avoid adversity

Wisdom is essential more so than pure gold
The acquisition of which brings riches untold
These riches are not materially inclined
It does, however, provide soothing peace of mind
Knowing love lives in the hearts of the wise
Forming a barrier that protects from demise
The lifestyle you live should show the ability
To share with the least fortunate, enhancing prosperity

WISDOM CONT'D

The wise man's house was built on a rock
Taking no chance of one day being knocked
From the foundation built in anticipation
Of being replaced by people of different persuasion
The likelihood of planned gentrification
Which seeks to infiltrate communities of color
Must be resisted every minute of the hour
Maintaining living standards of neighbors of color

Attaining wisdom should be the ultimate motivation
Of ensuring your children has access to
And are seeking knowledge through education
Albeit wisdom is not acquired from institutions
But when combined with detailed application
This platform will provide the tools needed
To produce a child that is wise and well-rounded
To be able to stand up in this world and be counted

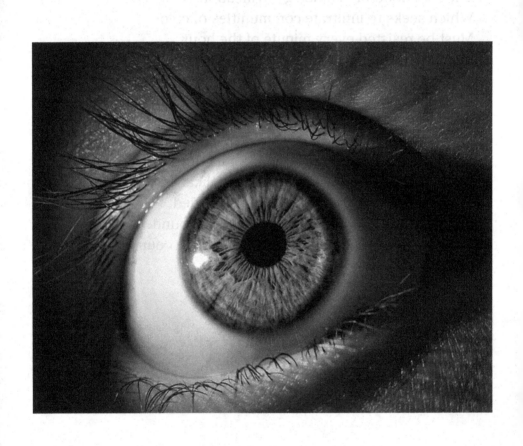

Vision

The power associated with acquiring vision
Is not a blessing bestowed on everyone
No one is promised this foresight through birth
This concept stems from having vivid imaginations
Sometimes appearing in dreams through transition
Other times a supernatural appearance conveying a revelation
Vision at times determines the outcome
Of situations or projects not initially envisioned

Vision is not what is presented through the eyes
It's developed in the mind through imagination
Vision presents itself in the abstract as in transition
Having only intrinsic form with no physical composition
Vision is the act or power of imagination
A supernatural appearance conveying a revelation

The unusual discernment of thought by imaginings
Gives rise to a mode of seeing or conceiving
The interpretation and eventual implementation
Of the details surrounding a specific situation
Vision manifests itself by bringing an idea to fruition
Which was visualized and put into action
Enhanced by the power of one's vivid imagination

VISION CONT'D

Imagine a many-times-rejected lot of land
Situated at a place having no conceivable plan
Due to the positioning and rocky texture
Which would require efforts of true measure
To erect a viable detailed construction
Satisfying the requirement of the picturesque subdivision
The eventual erecting of a beautifully designed structure
Vision and imagination being the key factors

Vision envisages no beginning or end
Your interpretation and action determine the trend
The actualization sometimes lasts a lifetime
Especially when it relates to the future of mankind
Specifically so the educating of your children
A real priority in their overall upbringing
Affording them the opportunities of becoming
Outstanding adults with morals and conviction

EMPATHY

Empathy is an expression of genuine concern
The act of imparting goodwill without discern
To a given dire situation or grieving person
Construed for a valid occasion or reason
Having taken the decision to interact
On receipt of which helps to soften the impact
When delivered with compassion and tact

Be empathetic when the occasion dictates
Showing genuine concern is an infinite mandate
Be empathetic when it is truly deserving
Recognize when an act is seemingly self-serving
Be empathetic without being condescending
Avoid at all cost the effort being agitating
Be empathetic conveying it respectfully
Ensure it's always done genuinely

Empathy at times may be misconstrued
Generating responses that could be considered rude
Specifically so when it relates to one's state of mind
Should there be actions, which are undermining in kind
Understanding an awareness of the painful feeling
Experienced by someone who is currently reeling
From devastating news or life-changing situations
Empathize by extending positive thoughts and actions

Empathy displays sensitivity, having experienced like feeling
Imagination or sympathetic participation is appealing
Substituting one's self taking the place of another
Walking in the shoe of your afflicted brother
Communicating in an objectively explicit manner
How the experience, feeling, and thoughts resonates
With that of the person in whose shoes he operates

Empathize by conveying thoughtful caring consideration
With heartfelt knowledge, of the gravity of the situation
Experienced by persons faced with dire realities
Sometimes a result of a lack of opportunities
Not provided by governmental and corporate entities
Empathizing can and will make a huge difference
When the recipient is aware the giver knows of the inference

Empathize especially when it seems inconvenient
Irrespective of the undermining deeds of the recipient
Forgiveness is key in the eyes of the beholder
Having the ability to overlook the misdeeds of your brother
Creating the building blocks for a better tomorrow
Where all mankind can live together and prosper
As was the original plan created by the Father

HONESTY

Important qualities determining stature
Are undoubtedly that of integrity and honesty
Which are the elements of a person with dignity
As life's journey rewards those who are trustworthy
This plays a significant role in life expectancy
It goes without saying in the current situation
Those people exhibiting these qualities and traits
Enhance and uplift an entire generation

Honesty is the best policy in this diaspora
Never elevate or promote any dishonest agenda
Let's teach the youth so they always remember
To be truthful and honest in all they do
Let's do what we can, reach that chosen few
So they can change course starting anew

It must be said however
There are many in positions of power
Who constantly lie, spreading deceptive propaganda
A means to an end in achieving their agenda
They have no remorse for the eventual outcome
Of division, segregation, hardship, and poverty
Experienced by people in need in all honesty

HONESTY CONT'D

In this dispensation, it must be viewed realistically
Honesty is the best policy in achieving stability
Which all people deserve irrespective of nationality
The right to life not filled with adversity
Caused by dishonest people who live by the creed
Of amassing great fortune, funneled by greed
Not caring about others who are in genuine need

We must break the cycle of impoverished existence
Teaching the value of honesty, by encouraging resistance
To the advancement of blatant and deceptive falsehood
Which is surely designed to destroy our neighborhood
Let's rise up, take charge, put an end to dishonesty
We can achieve this goal by demonstrating diversity
All working together to ensure accountability

KNOWLEDGE

Knowledge is power, there is no denying
The lack of which can be truly uninspiring
This being the reason why many are living in poverty
Befalling many persons eroding their dignity
Knowledge is the key to desired living standards
Sought by most families as their ultimate rewards
Make no mistake without this endeavor
Life can be tough and filled with displeasure

Afford the youth all the knowledge they can
Don't deprive them of the ability to stand
With other kids of color in the land of their birth
It's the only way to elevate and promote their worth
Give them the teachings that set them apart
From the unfortunate souls not given that start
Keep in mind they will one day ask
Why they were not afforded this important task

The acquisition of knowledge can be somewhat immense
Consider the alternative and the dire consequence
There is no doubt it's the only proven way
To elevate one's self to a brighter, more meaningful day
Not having knowledge at times causes woes
Generating foolish discussions, creating many foes
Every family should endeavor to make it a priority
So that kids may be inspired to enhance their ability

KNOWLEDGE CONT'D

Knowledge was not ordained for a select few
It is our task to make that statement true
The examples we set by acquiring this asset
Lay the foundation for success of which we can attest
By the achievements earned by those tried and tested
Becoming productive adults leading by example
Ensuring a generation who are willing and able
Having the good fortune of becoming knowledgeable

School of thought is that by being knowledgeable
Gives rise to the fact life can be comfortable
The lack of knowledge has proved uninspiring
Not having the will or motivation of succeeding
This is the recipe for failure and suffering
Being unable to provide for and satisfy the need
Of family members and loved ones
Knowledge is the key to success indeed

NATURE

Nature, the Father's gift to mankind
Not always appreciated, needing to be reminded
This beautiful world was actually created
With the joys of nature specifically designed
To lift downtrodden spirits at an opportune time
When it was most needed, soothing troubled minds
There is no doubting the Father's handiwork
Serving its purpose as was ordained to work

Nature's natural beauty
Mesmerizing, to say the least
Nature's natural beauty
Mind-boggling at its awesome best
Nature's natural beauty
Evolving amazingly as was designed
Nature's natural beauty
Coexisting with human life

Try as they may in attempts to destroy
This earthly creation with machines of war
Nature's natural beauty will forever prevail
Protected by the wisdom of its creative detail
Man's inadequacies evidenced by its failures
Serve as a reminder of the Creator's endeavor
Defeating man's vile plans, seemingly warped and hollow
Preserving nature's beauty for generations to follow

NATURE CONT'D

Nature's vegetation at times withers and dies
Being self-invigorating, springing back to life
With no help from mankind, no interaction
Evidently ordained in the Father's master plan
The creation of life not controlled by man
Yet knowledge and techniques achieved through science
Have man yearning, searching for evidence
To debunk the reality
Nature is the product of the Father's creativity

The beauty of nature spreads far and wide
In itself mind-blowing, where many have tried
To capture and harness without much success
In painted works of art, a true life likeness
Leaving them mystified, bewildered, and in awe
Unable to identify any notable elements of flaw
Immortalizing the awesome power and glory
Of the Creator, our Father, the one and only

Conscious People

This world is filled with many conscious people
Not necessarily in places where they are expected
Many have been ridiculed and ultimately rejected
For simply being from the wrong side of the tracks
Humiliated and ostracized by vicious personal attacks
Possessing intellectual levels superior to their accusers
This is common knowledge among the abusers

Conscious people are God's gift to mankind
Never exhibiting actions that are unkind
Conscious people are blessings in disguise
When least expected, providing pleasant surprises
Conscious people enrich befuddled minds
Commanding vast knowledge, seemingly beyond their time

Becoming a conscious person is not a personal decision
Having been blessed with unusual special traits
Destined to enter heaven through the pearly gates
Manifesting themselves through thoughts and action
Indicative of their desire and ultimate vision
Exhibiting selfless demeanor and genuine concern
For the well-being of others who are in dire need
While those in authority display indiscriminate greed

Conscious people are not defined by color or creed
They're best known for the nature of their deeds
Enriching the lives of sometimes complete strangers
Their endeavors at times attract imminent danger
From sources viewing their actions with contempt and anger
Enacting dubious schemes with devious intention
Determined to curtail their caring intervention

The thoughtful action and selfless generosity
Displayed by conscious people ignite the curiosity
Of interested parties with similar inclination
To provide much-needed assistance without reservation
Impacting needy lives, creating an affinity
Which lends to the development of a caring society
This world is blessed with countless conscious people
Making a difference by setting good examples

CHALLENGES

Once there is life, there will always be a challenge
Don't be tempted by the perceived desire to avenge
One thing is certain, the outcome will be dependent
On the specific approach taken regarding each event
Challenges will rise from many different quarters
The least of which may be tempered with laughter
Always exercise caution to avert hidden disasters

Challenges can be enlightening and rewarding
Maintain positive and critical thinking
Challenges at times are a test of your ability
To avoid wallowing in destructive self-pity
When confronted by elements of adversity
Challenges are the yardstick by which we are measured
Be of good cheer, refuse to be tethered

Throughout our lifetime, one challenge is assured
The upbringing of our children, we are tasked to ensure
When combined with morals and respect for humanity
Prepares and positions them to interact with society
Given the opportunity to be the best they can be
Leading wholesome lives, demonstrating the ability
To be respectable individuals exhibiting true dignity

CHALLENGES CONT'D

Intimate relationships can be fickle and daunting
Presenting challenges that take some undoing
Rife with intimidation and lacking consistency
Laced with deceitful tendencies, void of stability
Giving rise at times to erratic, unstable relationships
These challenges are however not insurmountable
Approached with understanding they are avoidable
Proven time and again, with relations becoming amicable

Challenges are sometimes born of fear and doubt
Keeping us shackled in mind and thoughts
Like chains placed around the hands and feet
Second-guessing every idea, surmising certain defeat
Garner self-belief the cornerstone of progress
Challenge yourself daily, trampling all over stress
Banish negative thinking, seek guidance and direction
The Father will provide, have faith and conviction

COMMITMENT

Commitment is a prelude to a given situation
Sometimes requiring different courses of action
Endeavoring to work through to a conclusion
Specific tasks with set dates of completion
Being guided by predetermined parameters
Requiring a detailed approach to the outcome envisioned
This commitment demands the urgent need
For strict adherence to the time frame allotted

Commitment to a cause can be a complex task
Staying focused is not too much to ask
Commitment requires clarity, expectations crystal clear
Taking the critical path operating without fear
This approach if closely monitored and followed
Delivers the desired results initially required

Commitment can mean assignment to a mental or penal
institution
Where one may be held in complete isolation
For specific protracted periods of time
This being dependent on current state of mind
Male or female it makes no difference
The nature of the offense dictates the consequence
This aspect of commitment can be heart-wrenching
As it does not allow families' frequent contact visiting

COMMITMENT CONT'D

A financial obligation falls next in sequence
Another aspect of commitment requiring adherence
Honoring the agreement, signed on the dotted line
Is in itself frustrating as there will be times
When funds go missing despite your best effort
Should there be no avenue of financial support
Irrespective of the intention to make good your promise
A sign of the times, in life there is compromise

Emotional commitment impelled by a cause
Can take a great toll, requiring you to pause
This form of commitment tugs at the heart
With your being depended on from the very start
It goes without saying, having given your word
Every effort must be made to fulfill this accord
Commitment affects all facets of life
Any segment not honored can bring about strife

PROGRESS

Making progress in life is the most important factor
That goal that determines achievement in the final chapter
Guaranteeing success and prosperity throughout one's lifetime
By positioning themselves to make that coveted dime
The means by which to make life a bit more enjoyable
Having the desire and drive of becoming willing and able
To support their family, putting food on the table

Strive for progress, make it the ultimate test
Let your voice be heard, no more no less
Strive for progress, break free from stagnation
Don't be derailed by the efforts of detractors
Strive for progress, endeavor to be a success story
Irrespective of obstacles, give the Father the glory

Progress may also be measured by specifics
Educational achievements earned having no risks
Failing to advance one's self by not exerting effort
Whether by your own doing or the lack of support
Determines the opportunities that become available
Should one be considered a candidate who is capable
To adhere to policies designed as guidelines to be followed
Even when minute deviations are sometimes allowed

Progress Cont'd

Progression is determined by the strides made
In the sequence of a connected and continuous gauge
Developing to a higher, more advanced stage
A requirement to be successful in this day and age
Progress stimulates the subconscious mind
Recognizing the effort made at the right time
Which allows maintaining that critical path
Designed to achieve your goal from the very start

Progressing in life brings personal satisfaction
Having overcome obstacles initiated by factions
Displaying positive qualities, never shirking responsibility
Designed with the advancement of life expectancy
Exhibiting behavior not projecting elements of truancy
Progress as seen through the eyes of well-wishers
Matched only by the acknowledgment of brothers and sisters

Imaginings

It is no secret, even stable minds will play tricks
Conceptualizing stupid things just for the kicks
Due to stressful thoughts and imaginations
Visualized by perceived and factual transgressions
Sometimes a figment of reality and perception
Which foster feelings of hopelessness and delusion
Resulting in acts of desperation and confusion

Exercise your mind with positive vibes
Confront all challenges with vigor and drive
Condition your thoughts, take it in stride
Guarantee yourself an enjoyable ride
Life-threatening imaginings can be frustrating
Strive to ensure it's not life changing

Imaginings can and will take a serious toll
On an otherwise sound and stable human soul
Thoughts flowing through the mind are not preventable
They are however definitely controllable
Determined by the actions taken of each respective person
A clear indicator of the rationale and reason
Resolving the situation with tact and candor
Never allowing imaginings to determine your future

Imagine a couple having a blissful evening
Of genuine affection and physical interaction
Retiring to bed with a feeling of contentment
Rising the next morning filled with excitement
Putting themselves together reminiscing the euphoria
Experienced the night before amid the aurora
Only to be accused of a suspected intent
To be pleasured by another, resulting in a distasteful event

Relationships can in this day and age
Fall prey to and at times be irreversibly damaged
By the imaginings of one or both parties
Questioning the motives and associated priorities
Fostering confrontation due to unsubstantiated accusation
A result of a vivid and misguided imagination
Imaginings at work, being destructive and demeaning

ATTITUDES

Attitudes, responses to which depend on the magnitude
When acting out mental or emotional situations becomes rude
The hallmark of a truly negative attitude
Responding sometimes to occasions that are factual
Displaying mannerisms seemingly not practical
Reacting in a hostile state of mind indicative of defiance
With emotional outbursts, which may be classified as arrogance

Attitudes are mental positions taken regarding a fact
Rebuttals may be well received if addressed with tact
Attitudes analyzed as being cocky
Lead to responses that are in essence rocky
Attitudes analyzed as being arrogant
Are best ignored and categorized as irrelevant
Attitudes analyzed as laced with hostility
Should be recognized as such and taken seriously

Should attitudes positive in nature be accepted as reality
When expressions of confidence are misunderstood as being
cocky
Projecting an organismic state of readiness
Responding in a characteristic way to a perceived stimulus
Whether it be an object, concept, or real situation
Which formed the basis of intrinsic motivation
Inducing an expressive feeling of personal defiant emotion

ATTITUDES CONT'D

To a positive attitude add virtue and knowledge
Temperance and patience serve to form a strong bridge
Demonstrations of love and charity forge brotherly kindness
Positive attitudes and diligence are indicators of godliness
Leaving no place for anger or being paralyzed by fear
Displaying a cheerful countenance providing a listening ear
Develop an attitude of not worrying over things out of your control
Seeing the sunny side of things, optimism playing a pivotal role

The display of attitudes seen as cool
Translated in that action becoming an essential tool
The perception derived of being laid-back and easygoing
Serves to eliminate barriers, removing misunderstandings
Allowing easier dialogue void of contentious suspicions
Providing a platform on which to synchronize opinions
Harnessing ideas with business ventures in mind
Another element of attitudes evolving over time

Attitudes viewed as negative in nature
Stagnate viable productive possibilities in the future
By dwelling on mistakes committed in the past
Not pursuing greater achievements, specifically designed to last
Deep into the future through the passage of time
Yeah, forging inner strength, assuring peace of mind
Be the best of who you are and should forever be
Displaying a positive attitude for all the world to see

Hypocrisy

Life is sometimes affected in some way or another
By strange events that we encounter
A conscious decision born of an obvious agenda
A result of someone's constant hypocritical behavior
Compounded by continuous self-serving denial
Leaving you with thoughts of ultimate betrayal
Not surprisingly instigated by a so-called friend
With the evident false friendship coming to an end

Be aware of the hypocrites lurking around
Making false statements as the events go down
Be aware of the hypocrites; some are really bold
Armed with lying tongues and deception untold
Be aware of the hypocrites; treat them with disdain
Exercise caution, however, as many are insane

Sometimes occurring from within your own ranks
Situations that were perpetrated as playful pranks
The decisions taken were ineffective at best
Where persons assigned, who could not care less
As pertinent facts were completely omitted
Which was contrary to what was requested
It's really amazing the hypocrisy exhibited

HYPOCRISY CONT'D

Hypocrisy can and will raise its ugly head
When there is a requirement for deception instead
Where courses of action should normally be
Consistent with that of those who were set free
The eventual decisions were different however
Because of who was involved in the original endeavor
The detailed investigation was somewhat intense
Ensuring those out-of-favor, harsh, and unfair consequence

Hypocrisy is a stigma persisting throughout time
Embodying the thought process and influencing the mind
This anomaly born of an obvious agenda
Visualizing a specific outcome of a concocted idea
The situation at hand achieving the desired conclusion
With individuals consumed by complete frustration
Having no idea of the required course of action
Hypocrisy at work, designed to create confusion

Signs of The Times

It's crazy, crazy, really crazy times
We are living in crazy, crazy dangerous times
Not one day goes by without happenings blowing minds
Mass shootings and random bombings with increased frequency
As young women and men seemingly void of decency
Snuff out the lives of their brothers and sisters arbitrarily
With hate-filled rhetoric justifying their actions
Indoctrinated by factions with warped intentions

Misguided and troubled people acting with impunity
Exacting carnage within the community
Enraged by hatred through racial convictions
Encouraged by persons of similar persuasion
Taking innocent lives indiscriminately
Only the Father can restore civility

It's crazy, crazy, really crazy times
With murderous tendencies on the rise
Where human lives seem to have no value
Be it man, woman, or child, the bloodletting continues
Gripped by fear and justifiable apprehension
Going to the movies or the mall requires consideration
Learning institutions irrespective of the level
Are fair game for those inspired by the devil

Yes, it's crazy, crazy, crazy damn times
Where life as we know it no longer exist
Of utmost necessity is knowing every exit
Of the places you choose or need to visit
Places of worship no matter the denomination
Are no longer immune from these vicious actions
These despicable acts are a worldwide phenomenon
Affecting every country, touching every nation

Yes, it's a crazy, crazy, crazy fearful times
When safety and well-being are foremost in mind
Replacing forward thinking in hopeful anticipation
Of a brighter future through goodwill and aspiration
Now on the back burner as survival takes precedence
With negative forces taking a foothold as evidenced
By frequent murderous acts committed with chilling effect
By persons exhibiting absolutely no regret

I Believe

I believe, no, I know there is a supreme being
The Almighty Father lives and eternally reigns
Creator of all things sustaining life with droplets of rain
Sacrificing his son for the good of mankind
With promises kept mesmerizing doubting minds
Whether it be positive or negative depending on the interpretation
Of those adversely affected by the current dispensation
I believe in our Lord and Savior who guarantees our salvation

Yeah, I believe in singing praises to the Father
What could be more consequential than to not falter
Yeah, I believe his teachings are a revelation
Take heed, all you nonbelievers, his kingdom is at hand
Yeah, I believe it's incumbent on us to trust him
We can do so practically on a factual whim
Yeah, I believe in his promise to someday return
Lighting up this world with his truth-revealing lantern

I believe children are on the rise, fulfilling prophesy
A child will emerge to lead, with knowledge and diversity
Having been enlightened now proclaiming advocacy
Regarding the rights of all people, no matter their ethnicity
Of equality, justice, and access to opportunity
Opening eyes that were wide shut through implicit ignorance
Forced to recognize misdeeds funneled by arrogance
A long-awaited turning point fueling compliance

I Believe Cont'd

Yeah, I believe in the goodness of man
Notwithstanding decisions not to implement exigent plans
Oh yes, plans beneficial to those in dire and critical need
Yeah, be it financial, medical, or socially unable to feed
The sick, malnourished, and indigent among us
I believe there will be an awakening of conscience and a consensus
Oh yes, to do right by our fellow man with the provision
Of much-needed assistance and goodwill in every situation
Eliminating lip service, which provides only empty jargon

I believe there will eventually be joy and peace
Which will come with a new world order that will cease
All self-centered thoughts and selfish interactions
Having been sadly woven into the society of nations
Most times subconsciously instilled in the mind since birth
Of countless individuals through teachings void of truth
I believe there will be a coming to terms of afflictions
Brought about by exposure and vulnerability to deliberate
concoctions
Fear not; the Word and teachings of the Father are our salvation

I MAY BE WRONG

I may be wrong, but I think this world is a beautiful place
The only problem are people with whom you interface
In their minds everything revolves around their lives
Showing no consideration for others and their strives
If only they could be a little more mindful
Of the needs of others without being hateful
Giving thanks for their blessing and being grateful
Seeing the cup as not half empty but half full

I may be wrong thinking the Father does not have our backs
That's wayward thinking; is there anything we lack
I may be wrong to think we are on our own
Why harbor doubts having benefited from seeds sown
I may be wrong considering myself specifically blessed
Cherish no apprehension; you are indeed ever blessed

I may be wrong; however, I think love will prevail
Despite the attempts of evil powers to ensure we fail
To harness goodwill, love, and affection
Among the brothers and sisters of our nation
If we remain steadfast, determined, and committed
Negative vibes and actions will be omitted
In the eventual scheme of things
As decreed by His Majesty, the King of Kings

I May Be Wrong Cont'd

I may be wrong, but I think there will be joy
Irrespective of terrorist acts to kill and destroy
With targeted bombings and shootings generating fear
Orchestrated by sometimes deranged former peers
The intent to reduce joyful living to a minimum
With the population in hiding, scared shitless and numb
Emerging only when absolutely necessary
Surrendering to the factions their freedom and liberty

I may be wrong, but we will be victorious
Overcoming fear and apprehension placed before us
Sing praises to the Father the Almighty creator
As he grants us grace, loving-kindness, and favor
Removing all obstacles created by the enemy
Clouding their thoughts, confusing their strategy
Blowing their minds, ensuring the victory

Inspiration

Inspiration is the mother of invention
Laying the foundation for innovation
With critical thinking, a requirement for success
Without which your effort will be meaningless
To be inspired necessitates an open mind
Recognizing the need to allocate valuable time
Knowing inspiration without the required commitment
Bears no fruit and stagnates development

Presenting itself at no specific place or time
In church, a classroom, or in a waiting line
Presenting itself through random persons or situations
Be it social events, grandmothers, or street-side musicians
Presenting itself through thoughts or practical manner
Inspiration is no doubt ordained and bestowed by the Father

Inspiration comes in many different formats
Materializing the vision through precise and detailed facts
Conceptualized by an incisive thought process
Capturing the essence of imagination signifying progress
Sometimes derived from misfortune and failure
Initiated by misinterpretation and conjecture
Eventually creating a rock-solid foundation
Built on knowledge gained and concise application

Sometimes striking like a bolt of lightning
When least expected most times requiring
Immediate action in creating and formalizing
The core functions needed to enact the vision
Brought about by the unexpected inspiration
Hasty decision-making becomes a necessity
Requiring intense and detailed scrutiny
Getting it done right and in a manner that is timely

Just as important as your being inspired
Is to be an inspiration having been tested and tried
Blessed with the gift of being inspirational
Comes with the responsibility to be motivational
Giving encouragement where it's most needed
With no desire of seeking to be rewarded
Inspiration is the ultimate driving force
Enhancing many lives, setting the right course

SANCTIFICATION

Attaining sanctification is where we all should aspire to be
Becoming free from sin, achieving purity
Which sets us apart to a sacred purpose
Unaffected by a hypocritical holiness-designed circus
Growing in a state of divine and blissful grace
Imparting sacredness that surrounds our space
A result of commitment having been converted
To a life of Christlike divinity being unrestricted

Endeavor to achieve sanctification
Irrespective of the efforts designed to dissuade
Endeavor to achieve sanctification
Knowing they will stop at nothing trying to persuade
Endeavor to achieve sanctification
Show strength of character; never attempt to evade
Endeavor to achieve sanctification
Have no reservation of calling a spade a spade

Sanctification demands a level of commitment
Not easily attained without measured adjustments
Which affects friends and loved ones alike
In unpredictable ways sometimes spurning dislike
Giving rise to sometimes unexpected reactions
Creating division and unwanted interactions
Eyes on the prize while being ostracized
Knowing the path chosen leads to being sanctified

Inducted to a permanent state having a religious rite
Should be considered an honor, not a right
Devoting to the worship of God by a solemn ceremony
Making inviolable principles consecrated by history
Secured from assault unassailable from violation or profanity
Treated with contempt and abuse as if unworthy
Of giving moral or social sanction to those who are needy
With lasting effects sometimes questioning your sanity

It goes without saying void of dramatization
During the process of attaining sanctification
Be prepared to encounter pointed attrition
As there will be attempts to weaken your resolve
By constant harassment and abuse, which evolve
From words and action designed to hinder the progress
Made in spite of the continuous demeaning duress
Endured throughout the duration of the entire process

PERCEPTION

Perception can be biased and annoying at best
More so than actual facts and may be a test
Stemming from the assumption of knowing
Details surrounding an ongoing situation
Taking its que from thoughts that were a perception
Hardly a reliable source to formalize a valid opinion
Regarding a current comparable situation rife with speculation

Be careful of the effects of abject perception
As to how it affects a given situation
Be careful of the effects of abject perception
Which seems to project unconfirmed speculation
Be careful of the effects of abject perception
All instances resulting in a prediction

Perception can at times be uplifting
One out of ten having a positive ending
Surmised from many such cases it was derived
From those with the knowledge of who had survived
Perception may have been garnered from previous occasions
Where success or failure was determined by revelations
Of factors that had affected the outcome envisioned

PERCEPTION CONT'D

Perception can determine quality of life
Dependent on the effort exhibited to create strife
Strategically conceived by a third party with an agenda
Of sowing doubt in vulnerable minds having no idea
This was planted with the deliberate intention
Creating uncertainty, eventually leading to confusion
Misinformation, misdirection, and chaos by extension
Are elements that foster wayward perception

Knowing assumption makes an ass of you and me
This being the basis of ongoing perception
We must make the effort to effect total cessation
The eventual end game being complete eradication
As the effect it's been having is truly concerning
Causing dire resentment, generating dangerous intentions
Recognizing the need to act, preventing deadly reactions

Real True Friendship

The term *friends for life* rings true
Relating only to a cherished few
Whose friendship has survived untold challenges
All of which in reality ultimately impinges
On the ability to withstand the ongoing scrutiny
Designed to tarnish the friendship's dignity
Real true friendship has no expiration date
The choice of existing being a mutual mandate

Real true friends are a rare commodity
Proving their worth in times of adversity
Real true friends are worth their weight in gold
Created by the Father using a special mold
Real true friends are there when needed
Even when their efforts are impeded
Real true friends will always be truthful
Especially when it may prove to be hurtful

True friendship harbors no pretense
Encouraging thoughts and actions of consequence
Always promoting positive and rewarding interaction
Ready to initiate uplifting intervention
True friends never participate in backbiting
Would rather risk a hint of misunderstanding
Knowing when the facts finally come to light
The truth sets them free and exhibits insight

Having no financial ties attached
Elements that always serve to attract
Undying devotion and gratitude in hearts
With only goodwill and love-occupying thoughts
A true friend will be tried and tested
Refusing to be found wanting and not vested
Dedicating their very existence to the friendship
Being a mutually rewarding and gratifying relationship

True friendships are built on elements of trust
This is the main ingredient and is a must
Exhibiting personalities of which both are genuinely fond
Galvanizes a seemingly unbreakable bond
Designed to withstand the test of time
Avoiding pitfalls set with coercion in mind
By jealous detractors with clear devious intentions
Of instigating the destruction of good relations

ILLUSIONS

Overactive minds lead to excessive thinking
Resulting with the visualizing of imaginary situations
The birth of which is referred to as illusion
This phenomenon plays tricks on vulnerable minds
Seemingly appearing real over extended periods of time
Having questionable reactions with thoughts of insanity
The effects of which are considered irreversible
This school of thought is sadly not inconceivable

Illusion leads to certain confusion
Try to be strong, never surrendering your mind
Illusion can cause lifelike delusion
Garner strength of purpose; it doesn't cost a dime
Illusion is the root cause of hallucination
Show a strong demeanor, resisting thoughts of crime

Illusion manifests in unpredictable actions
Sometimes limiting social interaction
At times consumed by uncontrollable rage
Which is expected behavior at that stage
Lashing out without provocation
Deemed an anticipated course of action
This state of mind requires cautious approach
As thoughts are generated of space being encroached

ILLUSIONS CONT'D

There is the sad truth, by getting to this level
Suggests a conclusion of being inhibited by the devil
This perceived notion is without merit
With the affected person now expressing regret
Having been diagnosed to be afflicted by medical ailments
Which were confirmed by diagnostic components
Requiring specialized treatments being induced
With these occurrences now significantly reduced

The stigma, however, of being overcome with illusions
Gives rise to the thought of possible recurring occasions
The support and caring of family and friends
Serve to bring this nightmare to an end
Allowing individuals to lead normal lives without anxiety
Having illusions, sadly, is some persons' reality
There is hope of recovery, by the grace of the Almighty

LIVING A LIE

Many a person living lives of pretense
Knowing quite well it makes no sense
Convincingly pretending to be what they are not
Creating a perception of what they supposedly got
Their expressions are mostly of the material kind
Other times having monetary implication in mind
Being completely aware neither are true
The intention of pulling wool over the eyes of a few

Living a lie guarantees no future
This serves only to diminish your stature
Living a lie generates conjecture
Leaving more questions than it does answers
Living a lie creates certain division
Setting the stage for internal tension
Living a lie causes real problems and stress
Resulting in a life filled with distress

Doing whatever it takes to create an impression
Willing to sacrifice the need of loved ones
The self-centered attitude so callously displayed
Food on the table or roof over the head
Are mere incidentals of their misguided aspirations
Acquiring trendy threads or attending costly functions
Speaks volumes regarding predetermined priorities
Evidencing a mindset of acute peculiarities

LIVING A LIE CONT'D

From the mind of a learned Jamaican educator
A fool who acquires a sporty Mercedes-Benz
Does not get elevated above his friends
Only now known as a fool with a Benz
Translated to mean, costly materials play no role
In determining status or ascertaining the goal
Of being a person of consequence and stature
To the contrary, now seen as having no virtue

There are those who would rather die
Than face the reality and stop living a lie
With aspirations of the finer things in life
Determined a must have by any means necessary
Intent at all cost to outdo their adversary
Showing no concern for those hurt in the process
Doing whatever it takes to gain complete access
To what they conceive as important to impress
That element of society seen as undesirable at best

HOME

Home, the place that should provide tranquility
When at all other places there is adversity
After a hard day hitting the daily grind
This should be one sure place to relax and unwind
Clubs and bars should never take the place
Of the home where there should be solace
This must be the place to find peace and contentment
Never having situations leading to appeasement

Home, a place of joy and happiness
The only place designed to relieve stress
Home, a place of fulfillment void of duress
The place where there should be no resentment
Home, a place of love and commitment
The place where you should receive loving treatment
Home, a place of unabashed sensuous desire
Where your better half will surely light your fire

Home is where the heart is
We've got to make that statement true
Assess the situation endeavor to start anew
Eliminate thoughts and actions that contribute
To the presence of dysfunction and not being astute
Every home should be like a sanctuary
Providing an atmosphere of divine sanctity
Knowing loved ones are aware of the necessity

HOME CONT'D

Leaving home daily, taking care of business
There will always be elements that instigate stress
Simply driving along, you could encounter rage
Which can escalate should you choose to engage
Setting the framework for the possibility of tension
As in most working environment, there is provocation
When added to the mindset increases the frustration

With all these factors foremost in mind
Make sure your home facilitates downtime
Preserving your sanity with blissful vibes
Having good reggae music on your hard drive
Combined with love, kindness, and appreciation
Shown by family, friends, and neighbors in the subdivision
The home community playing an integral role
Bringing joy and happiness to your troubled soul

ABOUT THE AUTHOR

Rollin G. Mercurius grew up in the heart of Kingston Jamaica where his existence was molded by street-wise Elders, a member of the Clergy and hardcore individuals from different sides of the political divide. He took a stand against being divided and ruled, sought instead to be uplifted and schooled while embracing the philosophy of rejecting crime while expecting anything from anyone at any time. He worked at a Utility Company where he progressed to the position of Regional Commercial Manager and attended The Administrative Staff College graduating with certification in General Management.

Printed in the United States
by Baker & Taylor Publisher Services